Ironclad Beta
For The Coming PPV

CEE

"Civil war window (Godzilla, 3/8/1862)" was previously published in the CEE chapbook, *Obligatory Abe*, 2/12 (Alternating Current Press; Palo Alto, CA)

"The Battle of Hampered Crossroads" was previously published in the CEE chapbook, *Erasable Bond*, 6/13 (Scars Publications; Austin, TX)

Featured Model: Jessica Marie Barnes

Interior layout by Robert Louis Henry

Published by
Leaf Garden Press
LeafGardenPress.com

For every time Howard Cosell yelled into a microphone,
like the fight he was calling was taking place in the street

Zero

Hey, howza*gehhh*, nonfriend! Glad you made it. No, you're fine, you're just in time. D'ja relock the door? All six deadbolts? Reset the booby-trap? No, the moat was her idea—if we survive, we're gonna fill it in part way, and have a koi pond. Anyway. Hang out. We got beer, you want any? Yeah, I put out all but the marzipan, can you grab that? No, not yet, it's all bluhbluhbluh now, but soon. VERY SOON…

I love PPVs. There's no more social way, to throw money in the street. Please enjoy this guide as compiled. It's not so much about our two Americas and the donnybrook on the way. More a cautionary memoir. Of the first PPV, long ago. No film exists, of our subject matter. Even Thomas Alva Edison, was then, a mere stripling, turning scarlet at sight of an errant, turned ankle. History, well you know, is limited in its media, past a certain point. Which, is cool. I heard a recording of Teddy Roosevelt, when I was a boy. He sounded like a wuss.

Okay, set the Wayback's dial for March 9th, 1862. A Holy Day of Obligation for pacifists, or it should be. Long years before our greatgreatgreatgreats finished being thinned by the weedwhacker of two distinct Americas, a crummy-looking tub and a really boss-looking crummy tub, cakewalked a Virginia harbor, huffing and puffing and doing little more in the way of sinking the other, than giving the warship version of "the Marine push." The Monitor, brainiac mousetrap of one John Ericsson, and the Virginia—or Merrimac—or Merrimack, depending which Holy American Scripture you kneel before, were a couple of betas, protos, mock ups. Test runs. Battlebots for 1862. Seen in mindseye, I imagine they fascinated and frightened. Seen hindsight as object lesson, they might well have been plated in saffron. The Battle of Hampton Roads showed to Mankind, the End of All War. Relatively, the end of violence. No one was interested. And, Twain Nation, force-fused from Appomattox until after The Towers were dust, is twain, again. Don't run from it. The shooting's about to begin.

I live in my home, near-24/7/365. I prophesied this life for myself, in 1989, the 'why' of it, being Mob America a-comin', *High Noon* train. I await touchoff festivities in our TV room, saddened. What cuts, is that we're doomed by simple, asshole garble, the Silly Putty we've made of certain words. Many of you know my take on FaceFuck, e.g. **"friend" = you clicked the tab**. I have similar feelings, re: "equality". A mercurial mutation, that one, a Scarlet Pimpernel of a word. *E Pluribus* humans use it, switchblade, but unlike the backslash, "Nazi", *this* butterfly, isn't any fun. And, like all your "friends" who shoved a thumb up the picture of your shoe soufflé, "equality", has lost meaning of any kind.

Me, I'm all right with anal grinchers who are white on the Right side and impassioned pukers who are black on the Right side, as I can seem absorbed as Hell and be jamming to Hall & Oates, in my head…but, assuming Man, one by one by one, as a leveled playing beast, across the board…then, who gives a shit, about Armageddon clocks? The PPV of America vs. America, is simply waiting for some thrice-removed D-List Archduke, to go down, hail, Kingfish Long. Then? Battle Royale. *Between actual equals.* One by one by one, ya see. Mutually Assured Population Control. Rollerball Murder, eventually down to the benchwarmers. Pretty quick, even Ossifer Friendly and his cadre, going down, hail, because ain't no son of a bitch, gonna tell _____, they're under no curfew! Martial law, assumes a cowed people. Reeling it back to Lexington Common, we've been a "Fuck You" people, from GO.

Equality, yea, nay, twisted, spun, denied, split, deflected, projected, analyzed, demanded, forced, examined and a senator cane-beaten on The Floor, is papyri of Antiquity, for These United States. It's our Truth and Beauty. It's not something to ever be solved, but as exponent it proved quintessential, as related to warfare. **Equal + technology / ignorance =**…a push. A draw. Stalemate. There're more illustrative ways to couch it, but "Mexican standoff" defeats my point by appearing to side, and I can't keep citing Actual *Trek*'s "Lazarus and Lazarus", or I'm gonna get a phone call. I'd refer to something 90's, called a "Stasis Deck", but that's an even *worse* phone call. So, uhh…try and imagine our two Americas, "Twain Nation" as I call it, as two immortals in the middle of a meadow, trying to murder one another, with swords made of Nerf. Now, change only the word, "Nerf". The coming PPV, on deck right after the Schaefer ads, is unwinnable slaughter *as unwinnable*, due to Equality.

The Monitor and Merrimac, were ships built on an amazing new principle of "iron sinks wood" (WTF?), but otherwise, had as much in common as you and the shittiest date you ever met…yet, the one naval battle of our (so far) one Civil War which anyone can call up if pressed, was a slow, lumbering, clumsy, dinosaurs do The Bump, no one-hurt-no one object lesson. Naval historians, lazy to a man, yaddayadda only The New Era brought by these chugalugs. Never the object lesson… probably because war historians are rarely vocal pacifists, and The Battle of Hampton Roads, was poster skirmish for Unilateral Disarmament. In short, Equal vs. Equal, removing the zig vs. zag of human error as much as can…you have Nothing Occurring. It wasn't only wooden men o' war and Pegleg Pete the ironclads erased. The four-hour, really sloppy bar fight off Newport News, wasn't "The World Has Advanced" nor "Our World Is More Dangerous". It was "Perfect Equality Ends Conflict". This statement is not hawkish, btw. It's as dove as "Joshua", at the end of *Wargames*…which, I better not pay out with, either. Last line. Dramatic cheat. Legal people. Not good.

Let's step out of the Wayback Machine and sit on the dock of the bay, Otis. As we wait for those in the Red Corner and those in the Blue Corner to makeover *E Pluribus* into a Kevin Costner vehicle, watch what happens, when machines try it. You'll wonder why further munitions got built. The original Fat Man and Little Boy, could have been our last. They weren't, because back at the PPV, 21st Century, we have a slightly different problem. Man thinks. And, he bleeds. And then, he fights about both.

Let's watch the iron boats, drunks in an alley, reeling about, and you'll see what happens, when everyone has the same technology. It ain't no tons of fun from Avalon Hill. That it's never ended, proves Man is Cain as intrinsic. And, Man likes that. A whole, big bunch.

And, I like marzipan, so it's the Apocalyptic PPV, only in Two Americas, Next—right after this Special Feature.

CEE,
relaxing in the wardroom,
Skylab, July 11th, 1979

3

7346. Monitor and Merrimac Building, Elitch's Gardens, Denver, Colo.

BATTLE of THE MONITOR AND MERRIMAC

Battery Hollywood

And being a supermarket display figure, is fantastic

Of course, entertainment
Required far less to entertain
In salad days of Dana Carvey's "Grumpy Old Man"
It's how things like mumbletypeg
Or talking about what a cloud looks like
Or spying with your little eye
Or duels at dawn
Were a perfectly normal Order of The Day

So, you take a hazardous tear-down build-up
Necessary crew to do the D.W. Griffith set bit—
As paying customers can't sit in matte paintings—
And you take your Kukla, Fran and Monitor
On the road
Hitting town, you maybe first, have a barker
And, the earnest town Mayberryambles, on in
Just as lazy and excited
Just as detached and invested
Just as human as they were, Then
Eat, sleep and crap
Human enough for You
You're one of Them
Not Dr. Lao

8080 MONITOR AND MERRIMAC FIGHT, HAMPTON ROADS, VA.   COPR. DETROIT PHOTOGRAPHIC CO.

6

Blind Hate

Jesse Ventura Vulcan-cannonade,
80's action, is not what we know
Of Hampton Roads, rather, exhausted
Old codger-speed, tech *tai chi* of
Mr. Burns making a victim "dance"
With black powder takes-an-hour,
Stimuli required, we desire
Transformers @ Madison Square
Really laying it on
Rocky and (Insert Favorite SOB villain-boxer)
The way-too-regal-acting god peopleses
In that early, Actual *Trek*,
Bugs vs. whoever ends up losing
Reverse-*Cocoon*, where only release of
HATE is "shared"
You get, I take, American personal imagery
Of a Two Americas battle scene,
Truth being mired, Hellslog, in
Chimes at Midnight:

Exhausted, mud/bloodsoaked knights
Rolling, crawling, vermin farmyard
Last ounce and No Dignity
They, who'd rather die
Than live as cared-for, a fed goto asshole.

Combat between the "Monitor" and "Merrimac", March 9 th 1862.

8

People Are Idiots

So many depictions, SO-Not to scale,
The match is made out as Ali vs. Frazier
People really gear up for it
People, Kid Heaven, Bomb Pop jammed maw
People want Hulk Hogan, No Time Limit
They want Kong and the T-Rex
But, the ships, were just…they were equal, okay?
"Equal", being one a' them there elastic words
Which breaks, stinging your face, GF fingernails
The history texts, old, new
Most always spelled it out
Merrimac = Andre the Giant
Monitor = Willie Pep
People, glazed, bursting John Madden, on through
With, "Yeahyeahyeah…" or "Yeah, Uh*HUH!!*"
And, default setting
Bomb Pop jammed maw, Kid Heaven

I can't fault fact-blindness
One is blind with eyes tight-shut
One sleeps with eyes shut tight
And America, Any, is a dream
Because if it's Not, our ironclad-god's UFC pit fight
Becomes lil' Gilligan, running dream, with goose
Between Skipper-giant's legs
And, *GOD*!
You don't laugh at Heroic Tales

9

MONITOR-MERRIMACK

FAMOUS NAVAL BATTLE

CAPT. WORDEN

COMM. BUCHANAN

'ey, Chachi, behb!

Long ago, Crystal Pepsi World
Stagefront lab, Miller discovers "The Rant",
Questioning WHY does everyone think
Everyone (*everyone*, in the whole *world*?)
Should have every opinion They, ThemSelves, have?

Without attempting to be cute about it,
And minus undue sociopathy, behb
I won't cop to saying *it's 'cause They're People!*
Or Orson, say, Man is a crazy animal
For, speaking for myself—
And, I keep telling friends this—
You can hold any opinion you like
About anything, any topic in the world
Literally, have it and hold it, from this day forward
For Right, For Left
For Red, For Blue
For GOP, for Dem
To love and to cherish, forsaking all Reason,
You can take whacko pastor-challenges,
And screw your opinions, every day for a year
Seriously

Screw your opinions
Just don't express them
Not to Me
They're none of my business

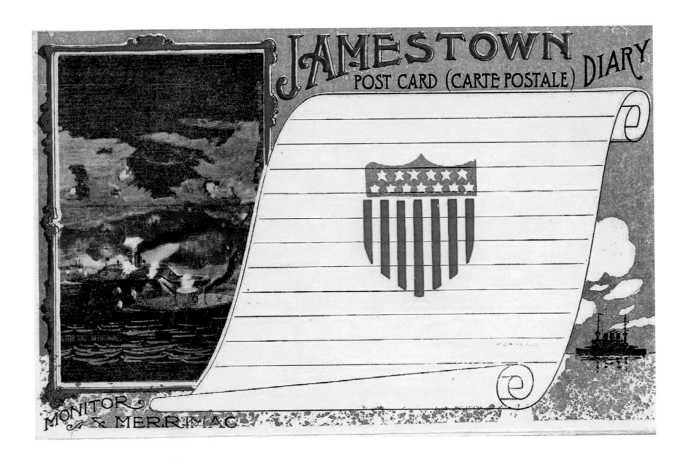

JAMESTOWN
POST CARD (CARTE POSTALE) DIARY

MONITOR & MERRIMAC

CEE as John Wayne as Bruce Dern

Emotion as valued
Kirby-era *Captain America*,
Cap practically shitting his spandex
A newly widowed, getting The News
As his cool, Frisbee focus leaves his hand
Just for a few panels
"MY SHIELD…!!"

Emotion as useless
Vampire Live Roleplaying
Bad actors with zero skills
Who converse even normally
Like they've had a stroke but kind of
Want to toast you with a rock
Can socialize, dead, as dead living undead

Emotion as offensive
Twice in five minutes, 1993
The miniature piece I paid *buchu* for,
Then paid for assembly, paid for painting
Paid for the painted banner flying free from it
Twice in five minutes
Knocked the Hell over
Like the men were reaching for dinner spuds
And, I reacted as a normal person
And, they're lucky I didn't have Cap's shield
Or any blunt instrument

THE BEAUTIFUL MARINE CAUSEWAY AT RIVERVIEW, CHICAGO, ILL., U. S. A., SHOWING THE IM-
MENSE ARENA OF "THE BATTLE OF THE MONITOR AND MERRIMAC." A GREAT MARINE
BATTLE SPECTACLE COSTING $240,000.

I don't want the fifty cents spent to begin with

This 1:NOT Lifesize show
Wouldn't have worked, for me
I'm not a forgiving person--I want what I pay for
I paid for The Battle of Hampton Roads

Ben Hur, all time, personal fave
I could listen to the Commentary, forever
On the *old* DVD release
Heston calls back the old days,
Half Jim Jones "I'm God" closeup
In that Too-Soon Made For TV 70's movie
Half old man at a bar half in the shoe,
So cool   *But, then, the new DVD*
And, of course, Now, it's 97% Others,
All of whom've spun the entire Milky Way into
The "Mirror, Mirror" universe without any actual
   Killing
(buttloads of Goebbels, very little Himmler)

Here's Chucko, way older, no shoes at all
God drifting out near Voyager
And, he's on and on about the sea battle
And the whatever x whatever "tank"
And as he talks on, they show raw footage
Of the honkin' ship models and waders
And, I never popped in the newer DVD, again

I hopped schools a lot, growing up, so
I've seen "Peter and The Wolf", five or six times
The Merrimac frightening Little Sasha
Is a lie from the Pit of Hell

Battle of the U. S. S. Monitor, the first revolving turret Man-of-War, and the C. S. S. Merrimac on March 9, 1862, at Hampton Roads, off Fort Monroe, Virginia.
It was here that the value of the turret type gun and the iron clad vessel was proven to the eventual rebuilding of the navies of the world.

Battery E Pluribus

Thomas Hart Benton
Paints the Death Car of Pollock

There are things that are Real
And things that are Not Real
Taoist filter, has it
"Things which are useful and things which are not"
Battles taking place in water
Water, boiling with blood
Water, which Would give Life
To The Ten Thousand Things
But, it's boiling
Had its mud disturbed
Got brightdull of All Color prior to acrylics
Dead and blood and crusts from ships
Brightdull, like colorization
Ted Turner Roads
Monitur'd 'n his merryMac, an old movie
A Nite Owl Movie With Big Wilson
Edited
Depicted as illustrative, as Realistic
Without the bodily fluids or human shit
No one wants,
See Humanity, the swell thereof, GoodBad
There sure is Happy, in seeing teeming Life

No, huh-uh, don't talk about that crap,
Jack Pollock was just sick, that's all

"Wherever it floats, on land or sea,
No stain its honor mars."

18

Tripoli Fade (shortwave)

Duhnt-DuhNT DAHDAHDAH, DAhdah, duhduh…

If ever you've been in deep waters
If only out, speeding The Keys, whatever, small craft
If you've felt waves begin to hold
Poseidon's grasp, becomes graspable as a g—
…uh, Daahh! DuntdUNT DAH-DAH-DAh-DAh,
     duhduh…

Even if "I am small", is impossible
Even if all you get is pissed
Sailing out, across a universe, which doesn't just
"give", no easing, a Hard Earth, Hard Nati—
uhhh!! Duhnt-dunt….AHH, DAH-DAH-DAh, d…

Half the Pilgrims died, the very first year
I doubt if half of half of one's family's half-siblings
Went from swapping fluids with the Indians
America, Now, is "you want to kill the last poster"
America Was…Hard, is all
A Hard place, Hard water, hitting you ba—
…dUhh, Duh-Duh-Duh, DaHHH!! DUHT-TUT-
     Tahhh…hh…

I once captained younger friends, into the Atlantic, a bit
I "knew", you see
Which is how Custer died
And how George Pickett got a horizon of men shot to Hell
…uhhhehehhh… …ehhAAHH!! dehhtt… …u…n…

4. "VIRGINIA" (MERRIMAC) SINKING THE "CUMBERLAND,"
MARCH 8, 1862.

FROM ORIGINAL PAINTING BY B. A. RICHARDSON.

AMERICAN COLORTYPE CO.

COPYRIGHT 1906 BY J. S. RICHARDSON

Civil war window (Godzilla, 3/8/1862)

The Merrimac blew the mightiest men o' war
To tatters, at Hampton Roads
A few hours later,
The Cabinet Room is in flip-out mode
It's Armageddon, End of Day, End of the World
It's War of the Worlds, and the Confederates
Own a Martian fighting machine
That could make the Union disappear
In a lot of lights
Richard Burton narrating
As "Forever Autumn" blats sadly,
The Merrimac rearing up all Toho,
"REEEE-eeAHHII-EeeaaAAH…!!"
Top American sober politicos, all ready go peepee
Disgusting, annoying
Me no get
But, then again,
When I got up on 9/11 and played my messages,
I snorted, erased them, and went back to sleep

Notes from the foredeck of Brit man o' war, as observing The Battle of Hampton Roads

They are strange
Creature ships from rarebit 'mares
Ludicrous
Hideous, in turn
This is not a battle, useless but as portent
But, portent is its shape, and that grim,
And the first mate
And the boatswain
And the powder monkeys know
This freak display of dark visions, this slop
Mud fists in a plowed field
Will be one day hewed and polished
As our finest beams, beneath,
Science finer than Figg or Molineaux or Sayers
Boxing beyond the deadly
Somehow beyond skill
The men laugh, as gross comic artistry,
Punch, as craven tin
Makes cathedral the doorway for ever-starving
Reaper

Lincoln's Axe Isn't Lincoln's Axe, Either

(drone of John Ericsson's genius)
(drone of Genius, convincing Fart Naval Brass)
The guide wants us to believe
This might-be-a-Lindberg kit
Might be really-good-indie
Some postwar petty officer's hobby
Who knows   He Don't
This ISN'T the model Ericsson showed
Those stuffy children of Valley Forge
(drone of tortured genius)
(drone of Ericsson as Jerry Lewis of The Sea)
No one ever calls him on this?
I have a bit of an eye, I can see the materials
The composition of its essential nomenclature
Jesus! Is that pilot house styrene?
So…Ben Franklin started
The chain "Ben Franklin", maybe?
This is sad
Thiz just shit
And, if I call him on it, I'm *the asshole*
As he'll yodel, Nelson Eddy, about the "symbol"

And double-digit IQ tour group, already thinking
"Complimentary buffet"
Will hate my fucking-guts, for lying
And for telling the Truth

MONITOR AND MERRIMAC—RIVERVIEW—1909

He Sits at the Left Hand of The Father

Article, Election Year, 1980
Warning to those who championed
The Gipper
As, "he'll sure fix 'Their' wagon"
Warning, as, "YEAH…YOURS, TOO"
Teddy Roosevelt's big stick
Was not a rocket launcher
But a supermarket broom, wide as the sky

Word to pretend "alpha"-males of Today:
The Brute as alpha
Knows you're holding the rock
You won't get the chance to toast him,
"Alpha", actual, is Captain Everything still The Brute
I understand every man thinks he's figured out
The Fucking-Universe and how to hitchhike, but
Well
Sick as it sounds
I'd like to watch you each explain it,
Know-It-All,
Electrode,
At Gitmo

FIGHT BETWEEN "MONITOR AND MERRIMAC",
A DECIDING NAVAL ENGAGEMENT OF THE CIVIL WAR.

103850

Pass the Coconut Beer Shrimp (w/Indian marmalade)

Likewise, robot of Cus D'Amato
Satisfied, bar, nachos, very 80s
We bang a nod as howl, howl approval Seal
Approve unstoppable 'bot
Whom nothing and no one can stand before
Iron as our Teflon
80s, solid, expected perfection, push-button
Watching the automatic, laughing baby doll
Cool, until, one night
'Bot smashes the wrong victim

"Wrong"?
But, Isaac Asimov *made up* his "rules"
"Rules"?
You cannot presuppose
You cannot "make"
You can only punish
And, not You

We're all for Self as the insane old wretch
In the "pterodactyl" *Jonny Quest*
"KILL, Turu! KILL!", we tell Our champions
Oh, him go SMASH, we so proud!
No
No, n'nono

THE FIRST NAVAL CONFLICT BETWEEN IRON CLAD VESSELS, IN HAMPTON ROADS, MARCH 9TH, 1862 IN SIGHT OF HOTEL CHAMBERLIN, GEO. F. ADAMS, MGR., FORTRESS MONROE, VA.

Monument Avenue, Richmond

Before you bow, open-toe
To statue of Lee,
Ask him this simple question:
"What Have You Done For Me Lately?"
And, when he doesn't answer,
Move to the Middle East
Move somewhere, anywhere on Earth
Allowed free-range rage
Without some bogus, grannyish "science"
Becoming involved

Battery Sinai

Navajos Wrote The Vulgate, Jerome

Good to see this pitcher
This ole pitcher inna ole book
Like the ole one I got on Algeria
In French
With every scimitar-heavy,
Graham Chapman hiding from the Romans
Hey, there's the Gospel of Barnabas on the ground!
Palm camel minaret AESOP's wet dream
Bundled Happy Happy *Joyeux Joyeux, Viva de Gaulle!*
Lotsa ole pitchers fer showin' 'n schoolin'
Gramma stuff, she'd've loved this
RAMBO was new, when she died,
Love this ole tome, 's like the one I got
On Indochina
In French
Lather, rinse, repeat with score from *Platoon*,
This book, this ole informative cuddle monster
's like a big, long, detailed Civil War naval copy
Of a Daguerreotype I saw, of Hadrian's Arch
The exact, same godstuff, suffusing
The exact, same "through a glass darkly"

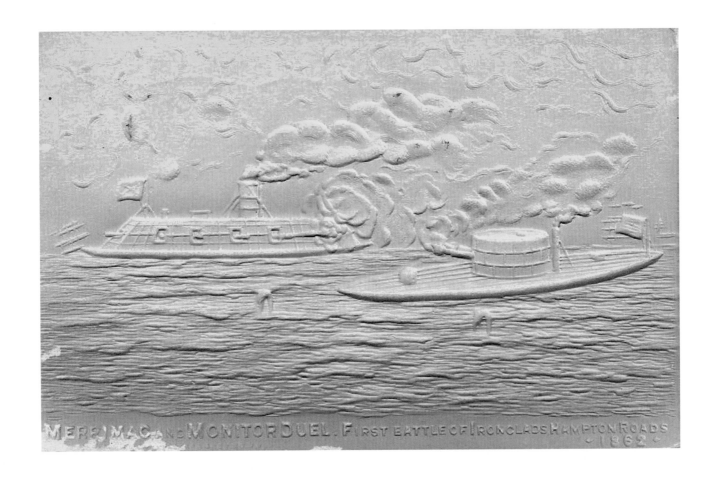

MERRIMAC AND MONITOR DUEL. FIRST BATTLE OF IRONCLADS HAMPTON ROADS 1862

34

Oh, Mr. Roddenberry...! Oh, Mr. Sartre...!

Ignoring all faith issues, or those, re: "what is spirit"
I can actually imagine
Being locked in limited space
Locked, encased, entrapped, a cell of sorts
With *A* nemesis from this life
(believe me, I've had plenty)
I can even imagine
And have, and have written stories
Of limited, mortal Hells of the flesh
Places dark and close of space, of no escape
Subhuman-level cage match of an I Guy and _____
I can imagine a hopeless, endless, mindless
Combat
It's easy to call up images of mutual torture and
Suffering,

Almost sexual hatred and "gnashing of teeth"
…but…IF such, it's foolish to assume we choose
Either opponent or terms of said Eternity
And…that'd be ETERNITY
Not some "Hate Love Boat" flagellation
Eternity, with everything extraneous sucked away, is

You're Just There   And, the Other is There
And, money don't talk and (okay, you get it)

I love mySelf enough, I understand
Why many Others, Hate Christianity,
Others, Hate themSelves
And, the Lovecraftian horror of Christianity, is
Ain't no such thing as "Not"

5. "VIRGINIA" (MERRIMAC) IN BATTLE WITH THE "MONITOR" IN HAMPTON ROADS, MARCH 9, 1862.

FROM ORIGINAL PAINTING BY B. A. RICHARDSON.

36

The Papal States and The Ottoman Turks

Opposites don't attract
The idea that they do, is a myth
But, then, of course, some someones
Want to play The Good Maria, from Fritz Lang's
Metropolis
Joining hands of opposition, Man as group therapy
Again, a contrived Christ,
Which is Any tenth-rate Christ's
Own issues,
It has about as much to do with unity, love,
Togetherness, understanding and
Dancing all-Whoville, around a mulberry bush

As local, candied photo ops make my home burgh
The Emerald City
Like the *South Park*, where the gangs of colors
"get it", due to social Big Bang of "hey…*c'mon*…"
C'mon…
Nuance, is something almost wholly removed
From peoples, even your grands
Microbes, to within a couple gens back
Nuance, newer than you know, is not a magic powder
It's the fruit of The Knowledge of Good and Evil
It's some, being a NASCAR tragedy, flying stands
It's most, as football players, dancing electric
On m'brother's Cold War cold metal rahrah field

A Friend of God, Postulates

The Douay-Rheims, calls The Book of Revelation
"The Apocalypse"
A term even "moon any notion of deity" *volk*
Can get behind, pardon the pun
But if you peer out your MAIL slot,
You see a world full of exoskeletons
Entrapping rhino hides
Ostensibly for protection
But used in action as Black Knight gear for
"Have Atchoo!"
People, effectively, and I've said this, before
People, are composed of water, and
Three or four lbs. of jade
So, whether Apocalypse of Douay-Rheims
Or, Revelation of Scofield
I've gone blind to any notion
Of The World as beholding a King of Kings
Automatically responding with awe and cower
Even given a few nations and whole groups zapped
(which assumes a Salem Kirban-God, but)
I can't see Earth as masses as the multitudes
Having anything but the need
To ralph random minds at YHWH

If, say, oh, hypothetically, they found out that
He smoked

(We are experiencing technical difficulties—Please Stand By)

Daniel and Chester's French Workshop (Public Access)

(power drill, pressure-whine; hammer, pounding)
"I don't want—"

"—as in, 'Everywhere'!"
(wrench dropped)

"Got the ma--?"
(hammer, erratic)
"—maybe take him—"
(drill dry-tested, then applied)

"—gonna say!"
"Well, if it's wha—"
(wooden dowels dropped; hammer, hard strike)

(drill, high-whining)
"Maybe I'm ha—"
"—do — for you!"

(tire gun applied, efficient use)

"I'm gonna sna—!"

(voiceover): You're reading CEE, the Poetic Community's Most-Published Secret....

41

Battery Symbiosis

The Battle of Hampered Crossroads
(Ironclad Selves)

Wind and water
Pierced by hotshot
Our tears
I, ignorant hogfat casemate
You, cold cheesebox of dark
Unknowable, closed off, we
See out but to
Damage
Hurting, marring,
Ugly-ing
But never to purpose
Never getting through
Only
Wind and water
Pierced by
"What about me?"

2. "MERR.MAC" IN DRY DOCK, BEING CONVERTED INTO
THE IRON BATTERY "VIRGINIA."

FROM ORIGINAL PAINTING BY B. A. RICHARDSON.

Introducing The New Chrysler "Virginny"

Artisans, hammering in plates   tinktinktink
Sizes many, varied sizes odd, jigsaw ship
Brainteaser protection   tinktink, t'tinktink
Whenever can be rounded up more
Fitting hunks and dribdrabs available, just in
Tinkertinkertinky-dingdong
Adding to plating, passive aggressive
Slowly shaping showroom Homer Beauty in
Lack's spit and sealing wax
Whenever shipyard scores whatever, however
Probably a Southern belle or eighty
Rolled, mugged, raped for her flatware,
Which is antichivalrous, pretty 180, yep
Which, would be entirely out of character
But for gallant THE CAUSE as sworn to, *SS*
Even then, hypocritical as animal as mentally ill
With bike chains
To gangbang and brutalize
Primary Poster Excuse for your goddammed
Rebellion,
But, priorities? XX, 1862? No Tupperware?

SHE probably rebelled,
Gave "Ma'am, we're collecting up all the…", a "Go To Hell"
Denial of ape-morph past failsafe
"It's *flatware, sirs*…who creates scars for a human soul
For ten minutes of artisan add-on— – *O* – ###!!"
Tinkytinkytinko, tinkytinky-tavish   tink
Artisans concentrate on scrapbooking a battleship,
Can't think about the BDSM, right now

Battle Between the Monitor and Merrimac.   PAINTING ONLY COPYRIGHTED 1907 BY JAMESTOWN A. & V. C?

My owner's manual of my owner's manual…
(for R.D. Laing)

There is a look
In the eye of a human subjugated
The eye of Peace, despite all else
The eye to stay hand of Help
Because, OCD need of the
Post-Carter "historian", that of putting
"Everything" "in" "quotations"
Is what "help" is, or becomes
Saviors are shit disturbers, are miscreants
Looking for apple carts
And, if not buying?…look into the eye,
Look at the look of a human, as subjugated
The pacifying look you can't abide, the calm
"Ssshh…" of parent to child
This one accepting that wholly repellant,
You are not Them (what a concept)
You don't have one vowel, not even a "y"
Human is not cookie cutter
Rules are not universal
Law and Selfautonomy, oil and water

Procedure, pseudo-spiritual notions of worth
Are dashed rock, upon Solid Self
The look,
"It's all right, because I was nothing, before."
If there is a tragic flaw in the Greek Hero of
America
It's the very notion of solution

Civil Epiphany (*The Munsters* theme, plays)

I've said that action is control
That reaction, is response To control
That human relations, re: "love"
Are heart arm wrestling
Heart hands forced
By a Self forcing anOther
And, all hopeful or personal At Peace
Call this view, "dark",
Yet, if I stated same of *government* as control
Its manipulation, Its Force
It, punitive, making weak as proving strong,
Few argue but suits of Other of vested interests
Or ants unlayered, more plastic than all the rest

So…watershed of masthead of
Symbol flying, Castle Films, above schoolyard
Is the fuzzy tortures pirated, in *Videodrome*
Is the boot into face, described in *1984*
Is Ralphie's *A Christmas Story* bully
As destroyer,
But…this entity as included *individual*
On most personal, intimate level,
Is HTF OOP rarity, a legendary aberration…

Daily, street, affection, false platitudes
Nightly, bed, core sincere, felt heart, Real

…okay…

"MONITOR" AND "MERRIMAC". HAMPTON ROADS, VA.

Hand-colored

50

'1', is the most violent number that you ever are

When comparison gives way to contrast,
Screw what you've been fed
That's when the grapeshot
That's when Norman Vincent Peale, takes a piss break
And *Star Wars* and *Star Trek* fans
Are WWE, faces
"Tastes great!, Less filling!", an elbow joke to teach
Potatoes or stuffing, an area where a person's
Very existence is threatened
That's the Unfriend, nonfriend, in social tickle of faces,
"Who ARE You?!" Other asks Other as anOther
"Asks" being PC for "throwing down, Harley dude"
Diversity, has an Emotional Seating Capacity of
One (1)
Two (2)
gods, is intolerable
anOther, from motherboards, *is* an "opponent"
If It isn't,
Why isn't It You?

To all those hating on the Beta

As you bought this, for sober history
You downed the wrong load
I feel your anger, Luke… your thoughts betray you,
"What of the tenacity of Franklin Buchanan?"
"What of the back story, of Merrimac-with-a 'k'?"
"I'd like to see more of Ericsson's struggle…"
Yeah, well
I'd like to wake up from being passed out
In my high school Boys Room,
And scream joy into the mirror
But, we aim to please, so, as a public service
Here's Every "Ironclads" Book Ever Written:
Practicability
Practicability
Practicability
hogfat
Ericsson hissy fit
Practicability
The Holy Story of the USS Cumberland
1862 tech sucks
"snapping my thumb"
Blind Hero
Misrepresented Draw
Practicability
Sage Lincoln

This am antique eye candy and existentialism,
Homes
You want history, make it up, yourself
It's the current way of things

7351 PIONEER MONUMENT, Denver, Colo. The crowning figure in life size shows Kit Carson, the famous scout and Indian fighter, mounted on his favorite steed. Three other figures surmount the base, representing notable Western characters: the Miner and Prospector, the Trapper and Hunter, and the Pioneer Mother. This monument was erected by popular subscription at a cost of $70,000.

Bonus Paper Trax:
Three (3) poems about forced unity,
utilizing the American Indian

If we just shot anyone who disagreed
(Pioneer Monument, Denver)

Wandering through town
If E Pluribus was as in *The Postman*
Or *The Day After*
Or that *Twilight Zone* with Elizabeth Montgomery
Or *A Boy and His Sue Everyone Because It's All About You,*
You see icon, spreading tower of metals unsafe
Flowering fly trap of ideals which shit your pants
A Past that apologized not, its very own
Law of the Medes and the Persians,
If you thought you were Emma Goldman
If you thought you were John Reed
If you thought you could make a difference by going
One toke over the Mark Twain,
Pretty much, and *Unforgiven*-dirty, but, yes, Truth
You died
Not according, not usually, for Not kneeling
          To ideals you thought of as "evil"
For believing in Evil, as existing within The Tribe
By way of What The Tribe Was in the first place,

The Tribe doesn't change; The Tribe is The Tribe
Life is as Is, hence and therefore
You're saying LIFE is Evil, and We in It
You bring dissension into the circle
(Arnold/Bruce Willis/Stallone one-liner)
A SOUND OF BRADBURY DIDN'T OWN THE SKY

Union Crew Moves the Dearborn Massacre Monument (more shift #23)

Okay, everything's secured
We can roll in, maybe, ten minutes

I don't get it
Where to, now? Why keep hiding this?
Such a glorious waste a' time

Yeah, thiz like playing for Fail in a *Sims*
Moving it around, is a shitty compromise
You're just pissing off everyone, either way

Ehhh, there's pissing off, and there's "ballistic"
Melt it down or powderize it, some Red goes Rambo,
Put it village green, go back to "God Bless Our Pioneers"
Some Blue…no, trust me, Some Blue Does The Same

A PC Rambo?

'Not my point,
The thing exists, and enough people KNOW it exists
You guys want "shit or get off the pot",
Where did you Ever find That
When it involved people
Who, 1 out of every 17 Other people eligible
Pulled a lever for 'em?

The Fort Dearborn Massacre, Chicago, Ill.

55

56

Demerit System of the Heart

The boards say there's a lack of compassion
They say narcissism is, DSM, become
The Way Things Are
You can't Teach-teach but a handful
Outpouring of the heart
Not everyone is Ronnie Howard as Opie
Post-Freudian, most are a Hate Kid in a Chick tract
Or Original Beavis/Butthead frog murderers
…so, you won't live to see
The coming XFL-Universe, but, I dibs patent on its
Marital Equivalency Behavioral System:
So-and-so many "points" earned, per SO's demerits
Per bad behavior as (community standards)
End of the week, turns are taken (coin flip)
And, points are spent, buying brutalizations various
And, points Do Not Carry Over
…so, he either gets it together after he gut-punches her
Or Pilgrim-drowns her in the toilet, enough times
Or she gets it together after punting his scrotum, weekly
Through the ceiling

Or some ashen-eyed SO, bides their gauntlet
Until a terrible, awful, no good, very bad week of asshole
Results in Roy Bean movie freeze frame gunshot hole
Big enough to see Forever's clear day,
It's a system called, "People don't Love, anymore.
They can, however, BehaveLove.
Or, be dead."

58

Undeleted Scene Track:

Oh! Oh! Both Am Down! Who Win?

the ninja killed the gunman
flying death kick
the gunman had already killed him
shotgun blast as the kick flew home
both now dead, upon cement
I took their wallets and left,
since the theater had taken mine

SUM

If, Texas Hold 'Em player with work the next day, you now call, my cards consist of Barbarism full of Anarchism, Fascism High. The math of my hand, exists in the line of Spock's, re: "expecting 'sense', from two mentalities of extreme viewpoints", coupled with any social gamemaster being a thief from a den of thieves…or a patsy from a den of thieves…or Washington's Mr. Smith as contrived Christ, cooing pacification as behind him, Fagan, the Artful Dodger and the Manson Family laugh like Beavis.

The card of Extreme Right, supports the others, but cannot hold the hand…because, even house to house and no Fourth Amendment, you're never going to get rid of Smith and Wesson. Hardware *ala* John Wayne, is here to stay. There then can be no cohesive jackboot, which John Q. doesn't force local, upon himself. The ping pong balls, are going to bob as individuals, get over it. At some near, each hears his own voice, singing its siren's song. And, the Snipes of *Demolition Man*, guns down every Ayn Rand and Nathaniel Branden, who band against him. Bet me, nonrube. Vegas won't give better odds. If Karloff as The Monster had turned and fought, there wouldn't have *been* any villagers.

I was once told, by an admirer of all things anime, that the Japanese view America, as "a wild and lawless place, where anything can happen" and, much as I'd like to play the statesman, I concede the inconvenient cave. What works best, Here, bad, good, though it horrify, though some travail and others sicken, is the aftermath of Appomattox Courthouse, as One Nation, Under Horace Greeley: "Go West…!" Many did, Hell's Angels of their day. And the primitive, warts, cystic acne, trench mouth and all, governed. Mob rule as tribal, XFL-Reality. NeanderLaw. Thunderdome. Roy Bean–or the Earps, if you insist on nice clothing. The Duke's line from *The Green Berets*, "Out here, due process, is a bullet!" Perhaps Fort Smith, and factory line to the gallows. Best case scenario, a forced conformity to rigid, predetermined structure, Zero Appeal and nary a prayer. And, no deviation from that there template, Rimmer. Hulk hates puny lawbreaker. Hulk smash.

We bottom, at no one stopping You, except You. The Other, ala *mano a` mano* vid-games, armed, locked, loaded and indoctrinated mirror image, Equal…but, perhaps, in addition to weapons of mind and speech, they're funked out or pimped out or have worked out, so they cut a different figure; their culture, their role models, their entire thinking, their Gestalt, a puzzlement. The prof who wants to fuse us all as "one", comes at this from the wrong end. Sly and the Family Anthropology, isn't something innate, it's mere form, not substance, so, shove your lecture. I'm not interested in the findings of Louis Leakey. *We aren't living with Louis Leakey or the antediluvian*, but with One Another as What-The-Hell-Did-You-Say?! And, the Day is evil, and it's a hard old World, blahblah-helmet-punchline, yet I don't see any post-apocalyptic Leading Man, taking hand of Slightly Lesser Baddie, lines poorly written said in bedroom tones, as Not-By-John-Williams-So-Who-Gives-a-Shit score, swells. No, I see Douglas and I see Cash, because the object lesson of Hampton Roads, i.e. "Equal as stalemate", was lost on Man. ICBMs as Cold War refresher, couldn't impress it very long. A Kentucky Derby, Roller Derby, *I Think I Could Beat Mike Tyson*-nation, knows no stasis of "draw". A stalemate, being insoluble. Nothing being insoluble, of course. As Alexander the Great showed us, Once Upon a Cleave. #HINT#

Translation? Hurry up with that Dew or suds or your piss, your vapid phone call or meaningless text— methinks the PPV's begun! I've seen it coming, for over 20 years. We meet at crossroads, crossed swords, in faceoff. Terrifying, but as must, the unified belt, at last. Perhaps *some* America, will have its way…perhaps neither, then Red China will have its own. But, the bread, now, is baked by those who don't want to serve, and our circuses police themselves as though Marge Simpson were their maven…and, yeah, I know They've rewritten history, but I have a library full of How It Really Happened, and CEE Newsflash, nonfriends: <u>If the Archduke Franz Ferdinand, had never been blown away—and, scoff, I know some of you teach your crap, but scratch catalyst, and…NO WW1…thus, NO WW2…thus, NO A-Bomb, etc.</u> At the least, all different sperm, would have made a different world. The boys that swam best, are here...but, nothing is insoluble, right, and as Sensei Kreese told Miyagi, "Wellll, we can fix that..."

Okay, overhead off. Your damned cell, too. Got me the Cheez Balls, to start. I can hear Jim Lampley's voiceover. A gut-busty theme, DOLBY Surround Sound, flows forth, iron as might—*hurry!* Get da fuck *In Here!*

That's where I am.

—**CEE, 9/2/14**

"The Cumberland sank like lead. She was a sea of blood and bodies. But, her captain gave the order that, until they went under, the Cumberland would fire full broadsides in reply, useless broadsides he knew would have no effect. That's what she did, amid all that gore and death. ... The Cumberland died, but she died *alive*, spitting bile. As every text—at least, the older ones—will tell you, "she went down with cannons roaring." Like, y'know? "I'm dead. Screw you, anyway.""

–from *The Sinking of the Cumberland*, a 10-minute play by CEE

Made in the USA
Lexington, KY
20 May 2019